The Voice of Real

Stories of Who I Was Created to Be

Diane L. Mathias, MA

ISBN-10:1976079578
ISBN-13:978-1976079573

This is my authentic self.
Yes, it took great courage
to tell you who I am.

Who are you?
What is your Voice of Real?
This book is dedicated to all loved ones.
(and we are all loved ones)
May we have the courage to tell our stories
in the Voice of Real.

The Voice of Real

Not everyone is like you.
Not everyone will be honest
    But they will be as honest as they can.

The birds will sing true with the only song they know to sing
    While others may change their words
    Or the song
Depending on who is watching.

You are the voice of you, the voice of real.

This is a voice of love and the voice of tears.
The voice of who you were created to be.

               -Diane "Annie" Mathias
               © 2016

CONTENTS

Introduction   vii

1   Growing Up With Second Sight   Pg. # 1

2   Mountain Companions in the Rain   Pg. # 7

3   Synesthesia: I Can Smell Emotions   Pg. # 11

4   The Dog in My Dream   Pg. # 13

5   My Twin Story   Pg. # 17

6   I See Dead People   Pg. # 21

7. My Father's Clock   Pg. # 25

8. Invite Someone Dangerous to Tea   Pg. # 29

9. The Kiln Firing   Pg. # 35

10. The Day I Died, Part One   Pg. # 37

11. The Universe Within   Pg. # 41

12. The Day I Died/Homecoming Part Two   Pg. # 43

13. Blind Spots   Pg. # 49

14 What Do You Really Want in Life?   Pg. # 53

15 About the Author   Pg. # 58

16. What Others Are Saying: The Voice of Real Pg. # 59

INTRODUCTION

A friend recently asked me, "If you were in your tribe and felt accepted, what would you REALLY share?"

I answered that I would share a collection of stories I have written called, *The Voice of Real*. At some point in my life I discovered I was different and not everyone could "do" what I do. I have spent much of my life in hiding . But now I am no longer afraid to be called an intuitive weirdo or a heretic or all the other names that get thrown around. I hid these stories (that often brought shame) safely away in journals until the time was right. I think now is that time.

"Who are you? " He had asked. Hans King called out to me in 1991 as I walked by his booth at a show. I didn't know him then; he invited me to sit with him. I remember how deeply accepted I felt. This feeling washed over me in a powerful and fluid way. His manner was unusually clear and full of light.

"I write," I told him. I briefly told him also about the workshops I created. He looked at me with intensity and love. "Ah, and just when you think the world is not ready, never ready for your work, it will happen. You have powerful writing inside of you. Let it out." His partner soon showed up with food and Hans said to him, "We need to watch over this one. She is one of us." In later years he told me how I really must release my books. "Baby Girl," he said in his voice so full of love, "Others need to know how you survived. They need your stories to give them courage to come forward."

The Voice of Real shines light on the inner life of one who didn't fit into what is claimed to be our cultural reality. Now after all these years, I am sharing some of my stories. This book is for my tribe; you know who you are. Many of us may be hiding, giftings and all. I hope these stories bring you courage and inspiration. We are all in this together.

With great love, Diane Annie Mathias

1. Growing Up With Second Sight

Second sight is a term for a type of precognition where a person perceives information (maybe in a vision) about future events before they happen. They may know about things or events at remote locations (remote viewing). Scottish heritage is strong with this extrasensory perception. My Great Grandma Paul had second sight. I met her when I was small and she was very old. I remember her and loved her very much. She left me her engagement ruby ring when she passed.

My five-year-old self didn't yet understand that not everyone was like me. I remember as a wee one discovering a present that I really wanted was under the Christmas tree. I desperately wanted the Mr. Frosty Snow Cone Machine and there it was, all wrapped up and waiting. I also clearly remember my bewilderment at why my mother was screaming at me, accusing me of "peeking" and opening gifts before the approved time of unwrapping. I had done none of that and yet...I stood there, tears streaming down the same cheeks that were, moments before, aglow with joy about a longed for gift. When I came upstairs on that Christmas morning and saw the package, it was as if the wrapping paper became invisible and I could clearly see Mr. Frosty waiting for me. No amount of explanation would clear my seemingly guilty name.

My growing up years were very confusing. I had no one to talk with about my experiences. Over many years' times I began to understand that others I knew did not have these experiences. I would have a premonition or a "knowing." I would have answers to questions and be accused of cheating. "How do you know that? You can't know that!" I remember my mother's rage when I would find lost items or know who was going to call. I began to believe this was a bad thing that I did. I noticed others didn't act in the same manner I did.

I was a good student and I always tried to behave. I noticed things, even at a young age: I noticed how others did not play in the woods and talk with trees in a different, silent language. I found great comfort being in nature. Nature often made more sense to me than people. The trees and grasses and rocks never scolded me for being too honest or too sensitive.

The knowing of what would happen was confusing to me. Why was I the only one? Why did I know from downstairs in my bedroom about a terrible incident that was soon to happen upstairs? I "watched the pictures" that I saw and ran upstairs to prevent a suicide. Premonitions and senses, dreams and "hearing"... all the related phenomenon were often met with punishment. It was a difficult journey.

I had a very great love for God ever since I was small. Where did this come from? I am not sure. As a child I did not attend church except on occasional holidays. As a youth I sought to find the loving presence of God by following Paramahansa Yogananda. When I was 15 I had an incredible, life-changing encounter with Jesus Christ. It was beyond wonderful. I was also much relieved, believing that the Christian church welcomed people with giftings such as mine. And they did, mostly. I soon learned that I was welcome as long as my "gifts" did not cross the lines drawn by patriarchal leaders. I was, after all, a woman. And over the years and miles the rules became more rigid. When I sat with the elders and expressed concern about a man who would be taking over a church I attended, they chided me. Eventually all the specific details I mentioned came to pass. By this time I had left, taking my children with me. I sought to keep a low profile but there was often the struggle of "seeing" and not being able to alter situations. As a result, people would be hurt. This could have been avoided, I thought. Personal (false) guilt was often a result of this "seeing" for me. Knowing what would happen was very painful. At one point I told God I was "closing my eyes."

My walk with Jesus Christ and the other Holy Ones was not a part of the "religious" struggle. The companionship of the Holy Spirit has always been an incredible and precious gift. I have experienced many miracles. I learned to enter into the depths of prayer. I spent glorious time reading the holy books, learning from Elijah and so many others. As I study I understand how my responses to prayer were not strange or wrong. They just didn't fit into the ways of many men. I grew and learned, often with great difficulty.

I chose to keep my inner life hidden. I sought for ways to be invisible. To my chagrin, eventually it would eek out. Inwardly I still carried a great deal of shame for who and how I was. People asked if I could read minds. A pastor, decades ago, called me spiritually sensitive. He recognized some of what it was. Once, while he and his wife were out of town he experienced great difficulty with his back. I sensed this in a dream so I "went in spirit" and prayed for him. He knew it was me. Sometimes that happens.

Over the years I was "instructed by those who knew that I was blessed with these ways" that I should be grateful. If these were gifts, I wondered, why was it so heavy? I did not enjoy "knowing" things that I couldn't do anything about. I had to learn I was not responsible for the actions of others. I had to recognize that even if I "warned them," they mostly would ignore me. I began to learn how to be. But mostly I hid. Life was difficult. I had very few people to talk with about this, if any.

Well meaning folks believed I should never charge for the long hours of healing/teaching and helping them. I should "give" what had been given to me. This was often exhausting. I still had to purchase groceries and pay bills. Some people would actually suggest that I pick winning lottery numbers. That's not how it works, I would explain.

The struggle of living was multi layered. I had much to learn about living my life and the monetary system. The "Abundance Gospel" was horrifying to me. In my heart, truth was always about "Us," not the monetary fortune of one person. Years later my wonderful doctor told me that our world is not ready yet for my collective, world view type of thinking. I have come to understand that sometimes I am given a machete to clear a path where eventually, over time, a road will be built. Knowing this has helped a lot. We all labor at different parts of the path.

In my book, *Metaphorically Yours,* I explain a process that I was given during a difficult time. This unfolding understanding gave me the ability to listen to my own inner stories. While using this, I had a strong premonition about Hurricane Katrina. What should I do with this knowledge? Would anyone listen to me? I was so terrified of "being discovered" that it took me years to publish this book. In the meantime I taught writing classes, worked with the bereaved and sought to help bring healing in a variety of ways. I know that I am only a hollow reed who draws from the vastness of God. I continued on. I had always wished I were invisible so I could do the work without being seen. I learned to use a variety of ways that bring forth truth without being "seen." I was terrified of being seen.

My life has been a journey of learning to walk between worlds. I often knew when loved ones would be leaving the planet. I also "knew" about the new ones arriving and joyfully I would meet these babies in my dreams. I am a hollow reed. I am not the source of this information. I am merely a vessel, albeit imperfect, of Perfect Love.

Over the years, these many, many years, I have learned courage. I have had many "tough lessons." Where I once lived in fear, I now stand knowing that ones who belittled me, humiliated me and beat me can no longer hurt me. I no longer hide my poetry under the mattress nor live to please others. I have learned, step by step, to come out of hiding and I know it's OK to be seen. I am always safe to see what is before me.

I learned to apply truth to rework many misbeliefs and old paradigms. Recently my friend, Nicole Mignone said, "Your courage will inspire others. What if, when people saw who you really were, others in your tribe came forward?" I told her I had been labeled a heretic and a freak. Nicole responded with a brilliant question, " What would it be like to be labeled a heretic or a freak? Would you feel more alone or separate than you do hiding your true self from the world?" I knew these stories were rising up, begging and needing to be shared.

Then Nicole continued on with what I already knew but it was wonderful to hear it from another: *"When people are afraid of you because you speak your truth —and they see themselves in that reflection—that part, that mirror part—is the truth that we can only see ourselves in what we perceived. That is never about us, but about being the mirror and holding the space as others come to terms with the inner battles they are waging."*

And so here I am, standing before you with a collection of stories. I hope you will enjoy them. We are surrounded by love.

2. Mountain Companions in the Rain

"Don't crash," one friend said, as we all gathered up our instruments from the flute circle gathering.

"I won't," I promised. "I won't crash. I will drive safely."

I left the next morning by 8 AM. I had planned to leave later but I was ready to get on the road. The car was loaded; I just had to buy gas. The trip before me was a long one but I wanted to see my daughter who had just returned from Tanzania. The very good news was the malaria she had contracted no longer showed up in the blood work that was examined by the infectious disease doctors. The good news was she was home safe and eager to pursue learning Swahili. The sadness of leaving her newly beloved Africa was in her voice. "I'm so excited to see you, mom," she said. Cell phones make those conversations possible.

My nine-hour road trip was long and I was exhausted when I arrived. But we had a wonderful homecoming celebration in Northern CA. Loved ones had a gathering the following night to honor this traveler; we laughed, heard stories, and saw photos that greatly extended our understanding of our world today.

Sunday morning was my designated time of departure. I said my goodbyes and Highway 5 stretched out before me for 357 miles. I began on mile one.

I didn't listen to any music for a long time. My heart and head were full of thoughts and conversations. Cities and turnoffs flew by. I stopped for coffee, restrooms and gas. After a while I thought, I need another route. It was then I noticed the lighted sign on the side of the highway stating, *Traffic halted. Prepare to stop.*" For miles before me there was a a sea of metallic bodies, waiting. I looked to see a ramp within the next 300 feet, leading to Hwy 99. I took it, along with several huge trucks, leaving the stopped carnage of autos behind.

Hwy 99 was quite lovely. By this time, Jimmy Hendrix and Jerry Garcia had joined me. They often invite me to sing with them, which I did. We sang loud and soulfully, the best performances ever, I'm sure. Car singing is the best. I often sing with the dead. As I sung, I was aware of being caught up in incredible memories...ones I had thought I had forgotten. There were so many of them, and they came so fast. There were precious memories of carrying my children on my back. Memories of sweet honeysuckle vines and of a vase of flowers on a table, waiting for me. Memories of fall and the smell of rain. Sitting inside of a tree, playing music. Walking down cobblestone streets, being in love. Laughing in delight. And each moment remembered was full of forgotten details. I watched these pictures, caught up in this precious time.

After several hundred miles the 99 route led me back to the 5. I was soon to be coming up to the pass. The sky was black with rolling clouds. I glanced to my left and could see something out of the corner of my eye. This isn't the type of "seeing" like when you go to the optometrist and you read specific numbers and letters. It was not this type of seeing at all. This is the type of seeing that is more "knowing"... you can see it out loud, but if you were to tell someone, the wrong person, that is, they would think you were hallucinating. So often, when people "see" this way, they just don't say anything. We have learned, as a society, to NOT see this way. It's too difficult and doesn't seem to fit in with the "normal" scheme of things, whatever that means.

But I did "see" something. I saw beings, tall beings because they were as tall as my car, and they were walking along beside my car as I began to climb the mountain pass. They were walking, even though I was driving 68 miles per hour. They were, to me, somewhat transparent, but then again, they weren't. They were shining beings, and I knew they were companioning me. They felt familiar to me, like I'd known them for a long time. Then it began to rain. It rained quite hard. The lanes were full of cars and trucks, driving up a mountain pass, driving down a mountain pass, in the pouring rain. The car beside me, on my right, swerved. I swerved to avoid him. I then sought to correct my swerve. And then again, in a serpentine, to attempt to get back in my lane, attempting to drive straight, attempting.... again and again.

"Don't crash" I heard my friend say again.

"I won't," I said aloud. " I promised you, I wouldn't, " I said, again, grabbing tightly ahold of the steering wheel. In a flash I remembered being in a car, another time, and the vehicle rolling over and over again. "I won't," I said again, not slamming on my wet brakes. "I won't" I said, not going over the edge. I felt a protection. I was at peace. Eventually I was able to pull out of the skid and then the flood of what just happened, in full realization, was upon me.

Who were these ones, those beings that walked beside me? And the strong protection of friends, yes, I felt that too. I was held at that time, on the mountain highway, in a strong grip of peace that knows no definition. I was alert and aware. To an outside observer I handled the incident with incredible driving skill. In my own sight, I saw an unfolding of wonder. Even now, my words fall short.

I came home to find a mug full of beautiful flowers on my old dining room table. They were a full spectrum, an array of all colors and textures and sizes. I stared at them, tears falling down my eyes. Love had called me safely home.

3. Synesthesia: Yes I Can Smell Emotions

The first time I heard this word I was doing research for a paper in bio-psychology. There it was, right on the computer screen. I didn't even know how to pronounce it but the definition described me to a T. I read all the information I could find, gobbling it up with ravenous hunger. I read how synesthesia is a neurological phenomenon where the stimulation of one sensory pathway is involuntarily experienced in another cognitive pathway. I learned how synesthesia is a condition where a sensation in one of the senses, such as hearing, triggers a sensation in another, such as taste. Until the age of technology, this was commonly recognized in artists and musicians. A musician with synesthesia wrote *Rhapsody in Blue*. There wasn't anything wrong with me; I just not wired in "the traditional" way.

Discovering this was like having my name pronounced correctly for the first time ever. I remember writing an email to my closest ones. I told them I had discovered I am not weird. My brain is just wired differently. I cried for days .

Synesthesia comes in many forms. The most common is when people "see" (and assign) a certain color to a number or letter. Many people have this common form, although they may have ignored it, or repressed it, or forgotten. My forms of synesthesia are varied.

 I "see" colors with music so I play the colors. Is it any wonder that I love the deep organic browns of the didgeridoo? And to smell that amazing vibration. And then there is the ancient vibrant blue hues of my deep Cm Native style flute. This flute was handmade for me from an old grove redwood fencepost; this is my prayer flute that I use for ceremony. She is amazing.

And I will tell you also that certain sounds hurt my eyes. The very shrill high brass is a shrieking pink. Ouch! Some high sounds are this pulsing orange that is piercing to see. The only problem is I can't close my eyes to make it go away.

I also smell stuff. When I walk into a room where there is deep joy, the kind that comes alongside miracles and grace, I smell amazing fragrances of flowers. When there are lots of "legalistic rules," the ones that people use to micro-manage or control a situation, this is where I get cottonmouth, big time. I begin to feel like I am suffocating. And on and on it goes.

Synesthestely Yours

I am yellow:
I dance upon dandelions under naked sun.

I am orange:
I laugh aloud while drinking fresh humor
Drunk on hilarity.

I am turquoise:
The splashing is upon me...
Spinning with glee.

I am green:
Lapping waves of grasses on hillsides
Longings and roots and branches

I am indigo:
Morning glories grow upon me,
Tendrils reaching to hold me
My flowers open wide in the dawn to sing.

4. The Dog in My Dream

In my effort to "fit in," I rarely mention how I sometimes meet people first in my dreams. Eventually I will meet them in "my waking hours." To some this may seem odd but I've been like this all my life. And in some situations, this ability comes in handy.

I wake up from these dreams remembering so many details; the color of their eyes and how tall they were. I can describe them quite well. It's often a short glimpse but I remember outstanding characteristics too: brown dress shoes or bleached blond hair. It may take a day or a week to eventually meet my dream acquaintances but with these vivid dreams I am on the lookout, as if waiting for something really special that I know is coming in the mail.

I look past the lace curtains into the back yard in the early morning. "Look! There's a little pony in the back yard," I say to my friend who has joined me for morning coffee. We sit at my claw legged antique table and we gaze at this creature. My friend stands up and goes outside to investigate. It was only then that this four-legged animal comes up to the window to peer inside. His nose is against the glass. I gasp. It is not a pony but a very large dog.

The face of this dog burns into my memory. He is scraggy with such wise, deep eyes. He looks directly at me thru the window. Multi colored grey and brown fur swirls cover a lean yet very large body. In my dream I have the impression of a hungry one who is standing out in the cold, longing to be invited in where it is safe and warm.

My dream was so vivid that when I closed my eyes I could still see his face.

Two weeks later I was scrolling through Facebook. "Looking for a home," the photo caption said. A kind woman named Jeni found a stray dog in the canyons. When Jeni tracked down the owners they scoffed, "We don't want him. You can have him." Jeni knew that this dog had seen some very rough times.

Another Facebook dog lover then shared Jeni's request. When it turned up on my newsfeed I gasped. The photo was the dog in my dream. He was thin and yet his scruffy, courageous look was familiar. I knew this was my dog. I immediately wrote and described my living situation. *I can offer a loving home, I said. Nothing fancy but a fenced in yard to a home owned by a woman whose children have grown. I live in the desert. It is very hot here in the summer,* I continued. *My dog will live inside.* They responded with yes. They said yes! I was delighted.

Diane and Vikki brought him to my house on a Saturday. We were all nervous. Jeni said he was not aggressive but he did not like cats. She did not let him near her small dogs. No one knew what to expect. When he arrived, he was too terrified to enter the house. Fear dominated his large body. He didn't bark. He just sat down, frozen. I now had a massive dog that did not know what his new life was about. I named him Stryder.

The first night we slept in the living room because the hallways horrified him. He moved to a new spot every 15 minutes. We will work on this together, I told him. I too was afraid, not knowing what was ahead. But I did know this was my dog. Stryder had come to me in my dream. I knew that we were meant to be together.

"It will take a village to raise this dog," Diane and Vikki said. "He has had a tough life." These two gals who brought Stryder to my home lovingly created a fund at the local vet. They generously put money into this fund to cover all his shots, his neutering, a cracked tooth that needed to be pulled and a complete check up.... Everything a big dog needs. Vikki stopped by in her hatchback car to drive us to the vets. My foot was in a tall therapeutic boot, awaiting potential surgery. She and I lifted 83 pounds of dog into the car. When we got to the vets office, three of us pushed his fear-frozen body across the floor to an open exam room.

I revisited my dream about Stryder many times. I needed this dream to quiet my fears. Meeting Stryder in my dream let me know without a doubt that he was my dog. When he jumped directly upon the dining room table he was as agile as a goat. Now I was the one to freeze. What do I do now? Why did I ever think that I could raise this dog? There was a lot of work to be done. I remember a friend told me I was courageous to adopt a very big three-year-old dog. I felt better somehow, knowing this wasn't supposed to be an easy task.

The miracles continued. I enrolled us in a dog training class that was as much for me to learn as it was for Stryder. I was "learning dog" and caring for a big dog that was afraid of everything, it seemed. He didn't want to stay alone. If I had to go out, precious friends would come to be with Stryder so I could I run to the store or post office. He would stand at the door and cry for me. It was a mournful howl. "What did you do then?" I asked one dear one. She smiled and said, "I sang to him...."

The dog in my dream became the dog in my life. He brings wonderful companionship. He brings learning and laughter. He brings us a chance to grow together and to form new friendships with both people and dogs.

 Stryder is now a 95 lb. gift that I would have missed had it not been for that dream.

5. My Twin Story

In August 2006 my friend in Ecuador and I were emailing. I had told here that I had discovered that I had a twin. Her response was Twin? Literally? Do tell...

Yes, twin as in twin. When I was working at the hospital as director of Arts in Health Care we piloted what is now a very successful art program for cancer survivors. Art N Soul met on Friday mornings and every week we had a new project for our 2 1/2 hour program. The participants were told, "it's in the process, in the metaphor"... we had amazing things happen. Art is that way.

One week we had a project where we put ink on a printers

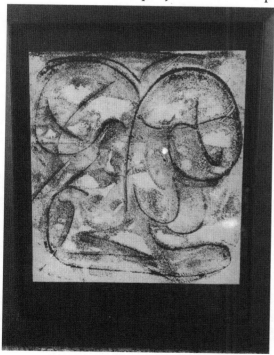

block, rolled it out (print style) and then each one would put a piece of white paper upon this slab of rolled ink. The plan was to then use your fingers and run them over the surface... not in a specific way, but in a motion. The white paper was then lifted from the block, many wonderful abstract type of items appeared thru this exercise. I did the example piece. The thing was, what appeared on the paper was quite amazing.

When we all put our work on the board to look over it, mine was, unmistakably, two little ones. They were in a circle/womb like thing. That was over 3 years ago. I put the paper away and didn't think much more of it. I didn't know how to think about this.

And, as you know, I have always written my "Joshua looking for Caleb" poetry. My wanderings and my searching and in that mix is a deep fear of being found out. That's always been an issue for me, like being "found out" about how I move in the various giftings. My dear mentor Dr. Kennedy would often ask me why I wanted to stay at the 50-yard line when I could go way beyond. I told him it was because I just wanted to fit in, to feel safe. He always challenged me on that level.

Well, in February I had an experience while meditating where I was really afraid. I was in the womb, and didn't want to come out. The short version is that I was aware that I had had a twin. But my twin didn't come out with me. My twin died. The doctors didn't know I was in there. They wanted to do a D&C. This was 50 years ago when there was no ultra sound. So it is no wonder I was afraid of being found out. I "relived" all of this. Following this experience, I began to put pieces together in my life. Things that hadn't made sense prior to this now did. I had been told that when I was two months old I cried all the time. I was hospitalized at two months because the doctor thought something was wrong with me. He later told my parents that there was no physical problem, I just was very, very sad. As a child I remember a great sadness that I had no words for.

In March 2005 I saw my mom in Washington when all the sibs came together to celebrate her for her 80th birthday. I asked her while making dinner for a family gathering in Washington DC, "Was I a twin?" She looked at me, tears running down her face. " I can't believe you're asking me this," she wept. She relayed the entire story, how she had lost the one baby, how the doctor, upon discovering she was still pregnant, researched out for information about one twin dying in the womb. She never was able to mourn for this loss. I showed her a small Xeroxed version of my art, she was flipped out. She had never talked about this before.

When I arrived back in the desert, I asked my dad's wife if my dad, now deceased, has ever talked about this. I was told that he had spoken of it to his wife, Barbara. "He didn't want you to know," she said. "He thought it would make you too sad."

"I've been sad all my life," I said. And now I know why.

I have come to peace with this. It was an amazing moment in time. Twin-less twins have many of the same similar experiences as I did. I had a chance to mourn for my lost twin. Pieces in my life began to make sense. This uncovering was a gift, but a painful one I understand myself in a newer and deeper way now. That's the short version....

Love, Annie

PS There is more, much more that I don't always discuss...I was given a dream shortly after the twin meditation experience and there was a black and white drawing of my twin and I. His side was incomplete and I remember picking up a brush and finishing his portrait.

There have been times he comes to me in dreams. He is one of my guides. He helps me.

6. I See Dead People

There, I said it. I even wrote it down. It has taken decades but today, in 2010, I am writing this in my journal.

That is my darkest secret that I have tried to keep secretly hidden away for all of my life. Ever since I was a little child I have been aware of seeing what was there, even if others didn't see it. And when I spoke about it, I paid heavily.

"You're weird," ,they would say. "You what? Sure... and I'm superman!" And people would laugh with great zeal and cruelty. I learned early on not to speak of such things, just like I would never mention the dark or the brilliant colors that surrounded some folks, or the suffocation I felt around others.

I learned not to hand out Kleenex to people who were crying on the inside, even though I saw tears coming down their cheeks. I had to learn to tell the difference between inner and outer. What showed up outside and what was inside was not always "seen" on the outside. I learned, on purpose, to "guess" differently than what my gut told me so I would not be correct and found out.

I wanted to fit in. I wanted to be a part of it all. And as a child, I had no one to talk to about how I was.

I recently heard a woman speak about going to see an intuitive. "When she was a child, her parents recognized her gifts and so they sheltered her." From deep within me the wail of a howling banshee rose up from with me. I was the only one who heard this, it was loud and clear. All my life I had longed to be sheltered. I wanted someone to recognize me and help me. Instead it was as if I was thrown into the wide ocean and told, "sink or swim."

I began to stuff down my shadow side. I did not know how to reconcile the intuitive, the seer, that one who walked between worlds. I lived in an outer world that did not want or allow my ways as normal. My growing up years were not based on mysticism but capitalism. My questions and curiosity were punished with haunting glares and uncomfortable criticism. I felt gangly and awkward in a world that did not call me her own. I tried, yes I really tried, but time and time again I fell on my face. I grew in deep shame of my authentic being. I wished I was unable to "see, truly see" because I did not know how to navigate thru the pain of what I saw. In my shame I sought to please many, I believed those who said, "God has given you gifts so you must use them for his Glory." I served and served and became exhausted. I did not understand how to say no. And no one thought they needed to pay for gifts so they took and they took and they took. Many said, "Oh you are so lucky to have gifts like this." I felt guilt and confusion because I did not love the "gifts"... I had a husband who was terrified that I would know what he was doing. And indeed I did. Those were the early days. Yes, I knew. I tried to deny it to myself. *Oh I must be wrong.* And one day I was so sick I finally had to seek out a doctor for vomiting and flu like symptoms. The doctor looked at me and said, "Are you under stress?" And rising up out me were all the things I sought to not see but indeed did; all the times I would pray that I was wrong but I was not.... All this and not knowing how to stand up and say aloud that which was real.

On a more practical level, I continued my lifelong struggle with the calling of being an artist/poet and being told at a very young age, " Get a real job." My creativity was not taken seriously. I spun around and changed clothes in my professional phone booth, emerging as manager, founder, professional... my eyes faltered but the inner sight did not leave.

It was the artist who called me back. She spoke to me and said, this we must do. And we again put our hands into clay, after teaching so many others to put their hands in clay, we began to reform our life. We will sell our work, we said in a whisper because saying this aloud at age 61 was to stand in the holiest of holy places and weep in this sacred space.

We will return and embrace our true calling, she said, this artist who never died even after being abandoned. We are strong enough, healed enough, wise enough now to live in our true calling. And the layers fell away into a deep pool where I caught my own reflection.

I see dead people.

I DID NOT, NO NEVER EVER want to be one of those who said that. I joined a spirit filled community. The Holy Spirit was easy and beautiful and I could hide in the midst of the miracles. At least until the men decided (because it was a patriarchal system) that I couldn't do what I do because I was a woman. Year and tears later I left, knowing this place I tried to call home was too small, way too small for me.

And the shame of being Annie is now starting to fall off. This snake is shedding its skin. And the new skin is soft and new and I look around and in my dreams "those ones" call me for who I am. They have called me my true names for a very long time but now I am not turning away.

I see dead people. It's not like on the TV where they are standing with axes through the skull or bleeding in gore. Oh wait...I did see something once at our farm. And I saw it also at a Zen Monastery, they came in the night, these old energy loops, and stood around me because they knew I could see them and I asked the Zen master if please could we do a cleansing on the land and why did the bell ring in the middle of the night? "You heard that?" He asked, letting me know that this was only allowed to be heard by a select few and yes, there was a massacre upon this land but no, no cleansing was wanted. And I watched the handprint of blood upon the large boulder and the whispers. I experienced great turmoil over what to do. I left and did not go back.

I see dead people.

They show up when I conduct my crystal bowl meditations. They just come in, these loved ones of my clients. They enter freely and shower love upon their living loved. Sometimes I mention they are there but mostly I do not. But I see them and thank them for being a part of that session. And when worship, true worship fills the space and hearts, they arrive. The ancestors, the concourse, the cloud of witnesses. They come thru the walls to gather in the midst of praise. They fill the room. Decades ago I watched and wondered, how can they merge with each other, as if they had no boundary lines of body? And then I realized that they do not. The spirit does not have limitations. Only the earth body does.

I see dead people, and a lot of other things too. I may not tell you about it or perhaps I will. It depends. But I am letting myself be fully who I am. I may not always say it aloud. And no, I don't do readings.

I am that lady who sees dead people....

7. My Father's Clock

It was Wednesday afternoon. I was in the bedroom napping when I heard the ringing sound. At first I ignored it, thinking it was part of the cd playing in the small blue CD player. I opened my eyes, slipping off the bed and heading down the narrow hallway. I glanced at all the probable causes: the stove timer, the door alarm that was not set, my cell phone lying on the counter. And then I found where the sound was coming from. Up on the top of the hutch, out of sight, was Daddy's old clock. It was the one that didn't work. The alarm was ringing like it had been for probably 6 minutes. I picked up the semi circle black plastic clock, noticing for the first time it also had a thermometer and a reading for humidity. I turned the clock over and shut off the alarm.

Daddy gave me this clock before he died. He also gave me a small student guitar that belonged to his father and his grandfather's framed Mason certificate. I'd forgotten about this little clock until about six months ago when I heard the same ringing. No matter that the clock hadn't run for 10 years. No matter that it didn't have batteries in it. It was in a drawer, ringing away. I thought at the time that was a curious thing. I greeted my father's means of communication with a wry smile. He is a funny and intelligent man. And yes, he did manage to get my attention. The same way he did today.

So Daddy, I thought (because I have learned I don't have to talk out loud for him to hear me), What is it that you want me to know? Barely before that was out of my mind I heard the name of his wife and her now husband. (She had re-married since my father's death) I had talked with her earlier in the day; she told me how her husband was not been feeling well which was very unusual for him. He had a fever and was shaking a bit. She called the doctor that morning and the doctor wanted him to take some antibiotics and see him the next morning. That was latest update until my alarm driven call.

"B. needs to be seen now," I said when I called her.

"We have an appointment for tomorrow at 11:30" she began. I knew I had to pull the Daddy Card. I don't usually show my hand. But right now, I knew I needed to use the big guns.

"I have daddy's old clock, you know, the one that doesn't work…" I began. Just a few minutes ago the alarm was ringing. I turned off the alarm and listened. I "heard" that I was to call you. Daddy is sounding the alarm. B. needs to get help right how. Please call 911."

I could feel her hesitate; it was disbelief and a brain trying to sort out what she had just heard. "I'm on it," she said. That's what she says when she gets something and knows that this is important. "

I texted my sister to tell her what happened. My sister is my confidante in my "seeing ways." She isn't exactly like me but she understands. She is more intellectual about consciousness than I am. Of course she is, she's the first-born. And we can be a great team. "Is she calling 911?" my sister asked. "Yes," I responded, after telling her I used the "Daddy's Clock" card. "Can you call her quickly?" She did call; the ambulance (and the fire truck) had just arrived. They were getting ready to head out to the hospital.

It's a funny thing being in my shoes. I was relieved that B would be in good medical hands. That shaking stuff with a fever was no good. And my step mom admitted on the last call, after I urged her to get him medical help, that his temperature had gone up to 103. That's very high for a man who is 87 years old.

During the evening I texted with her. Her responses were brief: *Still waiting, Dr. here now, going for MRI, etc.* I sat on the couch, aware that the doctors may simply look at B and say, "Go home, you are fine." Isn't that often what happens? We take a risk and then feel like idiots. This doesn't matter to me anymore. I wondered if the doctor would send him home and they would wonder why they listened to me. In these situations I always hope I'm wrong anyhow. I don't like being right because that means someone is in trouble. I have had a lifetime of this type of thing. And yet, the ringing alarm was indeed an alarm. At least, that's how I perceived it to be.

At midnight they signed papers to admit B. to the hospital. They put him on an IV drip with antibiotics. The next day they would conduct a surgical procedure to clean out the infected site, an area where a cancerous growth had been removed nine months prior. The surgery was postponed several times due to other hospital emergencies. When it was completed I received the call. "B has a septic infection. It is very serious. It is a blood poisoning. The doctor said if B. hadn't come to hospital when he did, he would have died. But because we came when we did, he is going to be fine. He will have to stay here for five days..."

Folks often don't know how to process this. Her husband thanks her for saving his life. If daddy really did ring the alarm, how does this fit into a Christian paradigm? Did her deceased husband actually send a message that saved B.'s life? What does she tell her friends in the church where this isn't supposed to happen? The dead are tucked away in heaven and don't wander through their daughter's worlds, isn't that right? And yet, it is undeniable.

If this hadn't have happened, B. would be dead now.

This is all an inconvenient truth. And here I am, her daughter, bringing this to her. The good news is that B will be fine. The tough news is that now she is faced with needing to find and embrace answers that don't fit with her current belief system. Alarms going off on a clock that doesn't work? Her dead husband stepping in to save her now- husband's life? These events rock through people's belief systems like Hurricane Sandy. And I was the one who got to step in and bring the message.

What will probably happen next is the story of daddy's alarm clock will be tucked away, out of mind, because it's too difficult to understand. Embracing that means changing a belief system, a difficult task. Our belief systems are often peer driven: we are social beings and we want so badly to fit in. How do I know this? Because I too would have liked to fit in. I would have liked, or so I thought, to be like others. But I wasn't. I am OK with that now.

My life has always been full of inconvenient truths.

I learned at a very young age that people don't like to have their worlds rocked. They pretty much like things to go along smoothly and follow what is predictable. When someone like me comes along and says, "What about this?" it is not uncommon for the subject to suddenly get changed. Or people get a blank look on their faces and look away. Inconvenient truth stops us and causes some to ponder. Some simply ignore it, others become defensive and even belligerent. I have been called names because I said something to help in an uncommon form. I have had to learn not to be pulled by "what people think." This was hard for me. Especially when I am the one who brings "inconvenient truth".

8. Invite Someone Dangerous To Tea

I think I am ready to invite someone dangerous to tea. I have been hungry for company of a unique kind. I am feeling bored by the thought of the average tea drinker... who might I invite? I think I will invite my twin brother, the one who died before we/I were/was born.

I know he will come; all I have to do is ask. He will be here, knocking at my door. Usually he arrives in my dreams but on occasion he arrives in the daytime. This time he will come to the door in jest and then he will walk through the door with that huge reflective smile on his face. He is such a goof sometimes. And he is very wise. He is also really good at directions. He helps me navigate on occasion; he turns up to sit beside me in the passenger seat of my car. Oh, you want to know his name? Hmm, I just realized I have never ever asked him about his name. Probably because we talk in twin speech, the talk without words... I have always known him as "My Twin."

I don't know where I learned to speak in twin talk; I guess being a twin I just knew how. It is talking in the knowing, mind to mind. No words are needed. I tried to teach my children mind to mind when they were young. I think they understood it pretty well for not being a twin.

Come have tea with me! I beam out to my twin. And there he is, knocking on the door. That is our joke. We love doors. Once he gave me a door in a dream that had a special peephole on it; he told me I could look thru that peephole (it was lit up, I still remember) and see into my future. In the dream I was sleeping on the porch and I was painfully aware of being too afraid to look. I hadn't fully entered into the house of my life yet. *Exactly right!*

he beamed back to me in metallic peach purrs. After that I began
to shift and tip toe into my life, one little toehold at a time.
Eventually and over a very long time I began to shed my fears of
being seen. It was a painful process. My twin was always here,
looking back at me in the mirror. No one else can see him. He is
very good at remaining unseen.

And so I go to open the door but he is already whirling around me,
dancing that dervish dance and laughing. *Fresh sage?* He says,
almost like a question but of course he already knows the answer.
He nods at his own two-sided conversation and smiles at my new
dog. Stryder is watching his every move, like animals do. Stryder
has alert ears and a wagging tail. Anyone watching us would
wonder what this shaggy dog is looking at. Me, I am gleeful and
watching this from various perspectives. I too am happy. My twin
completes me.

Lots of stuff, I say in twin speak as he glances at the piles on my
old oak table that is my main workspace. *Time to get those books
moving,* he muses. *All of 'em.* And he turns to me, full of
compassion. *They no longer burn women at the stake,* he says,
not laughing.

He knows the depths of my pain and rejection. He knows what it
was like to be labeled and outcast. And then he flashes to me the
memory of when I first began to walk with Christ and way back
then, the route of religion and coming home from a short vacation
with friends, that summer of 1971, to find all my belongings
dumped outside the door, my family home front door. I have a

lapse in memory about what happened next. I remember arriving home, looking forward to seeing my family after being gone for a week to Torch Lake and striding across the screened-in porch, 17 years old, to find all my belongings boxed and strewn along the path. At first I didn't understand what was going on. I couldn't comprehend this action. Wasn't becoming a Christian a good response? A step towards truth? A step away from dark ways?

You know, I can't even remember what happened next. I slide slowly in our twin speak. I project the picture of the porch and let him feel my ancient response, just in case he forgot, which I know he didn't. His response comes back in the form of that soft green compassionate hugging energy. *I know,* he replies without his words. *I know.*

I've been thinking about that situation lately, I return his thought. *I don't remember the rest of that. There is such a gap.*

You don't need to remember, He warms into a dim blue. In no words he communicates that he knows how hard I have tried to "fit in" and do what was expected. To fit into the culture of this society and to be involved in what others were doing. But that didn't seem to stick. Either I was invisible or horribly wrong. Like that afternoon in August, when my all clothes and personal belonging were strewn across the porch. The signal was clear. But where was the fight, the harsh words that would accompany such actions? No one never ever talked about that. Ever. Years later, as my father grew towards death and transition he asked me about my dreams and wisdom and asked for an explanation of how it was to have knowings, those insights that I would have and offer to share for the good of the family and the ones that he had mocked me for, time and time again. It was a lifetime of this and eventually I got it. I stopped. I no longer helped to find this lost item or that; I stopped issuing warnings about the family business and instead I sat quietly on the sidelines. He asked me for that information after all that in my lifetime and I remember just looking at him, saying nothing at all.

I am always here. My twin unfolds like a ripple in that love that keeps going on and on. I sit at the table; we are not drinking tea, only the waters of truth. *It's that rejection,* I sob. *Still working on that rejection for being me.*

My twin surrounds me. *I escaped all that, you know,* he begins. His words end at the beginning but I understand them anyhow. *You are very brave to live your life.* I look blankly, as if somehow had just asked me to pass the butter. *You are*, he insists. Again he grows tall, emitting courage. *You are the courageous one.* And now he pushes blocks of accolades upon me. They are of gold, shimmering and I am surrounded by pulsating beauty. I rest in the deep pulse of love, settling deeper.

You always have been courageous. You have suffered a lot for who you are and when you came out of hiding, there were many who became angry. They want you to be small again. They want to control you and for you to be like them. They want to think if you were powerful you would be wealthy but that was never your goal and that is only their paradigm. And yet now, as you stand taller and call in the currency of abundance they become even more afraid. They push and shove even more. They want to live in their smallness and they feel threatened. They raise their voices, thinking their wealth is power. They want you to be their healer and then say it never happened, proving that you are not worth the wage you ask. They are afraid because they cannot control you. But you never did understand that dysfunction. THERE IS

NOTHING WRONG WITH YOU. NOTHING AT ALL!

And then in a blink, in the silent drop of a petal, in the kiss of a breeze that is almost audible, he is gone. That is how it is between my twin and I. I stand in the room; his non-words fill the spaces within and without me.

My kiln is a crucible of magical transformation. I have worked in clay for 28 years and this kiln was bought for me as a gift. Yes, miracles surround us...

9. The Kiln Firing

I sit in my chair by the kiln
watching as fires burn...
It is the process of clay to glass
and transformation.
Watching that which was wrought by hands
into an external form
become vessels that hold
what cannot be contained.
I watch in the night.
Georgia O'Keefe joins the forming circle
With da Vinci, Van Gogh, Tesla.
The circle continues to grow in the alchemy
of this night
this time
this moment.

I sit in my chair by my kiln
watching the rising temperature and the fires burn hot
as the essence of creativity expands.
Soon it no longer appears in the form of known creative ones
but rather in the essence of unnamed and unknowable energy...
It is energy that I, even with my words
and my pictures
am unable to describe to you.

I can tell you what clay feels like, smells like, and looks like.
I can tell you what it is to become the art
and to become lost in the expression

I can tell you what it is to talk with this caldron of transformation
as I place each piece within her bowels
and close the lid,
listening to the awakening by fire.

I can tell you what it is to open this mouth of wonder
a full day after the cooling down
And look upon beauty never before seen...
But I cannot find words or expression to explain
The depth and width of the creative search, long into the night:
the why of artists,
continuing deeper into their art,
seeking to explain to others
that which can never be contained.

10. The Day I Died, Part One

It took a lot of years for me to remember what happened that afternoon at the hospital. Years ago I had a knowing...that is term I use when talking with myself. Others may call it an epiphany or a revelation, a vision or a deep understanding. This knowing came as I was playing a steel tongued Moyo drum with my friends. This particular steel drum had an alternative tuning that extended beyond the common scale. It was like scree, the vision that allows us to see beyond but on that day the "seeing" wasn't with my eyes. I looked out across the sound. My conscious mind blanked out and a download came into me like the unfurling of a zip drive. I blinked and knew at that moment that years prior I had actually "died" during my gall bladder surgery.

Before this moment on the Moyo drum I already knew this:

I knew that before the surgery I saw my deceased father standing in the corner, leaning up against a wall just before the anesthesiologist came in.

I remember after the surgery the nurse peering at me, saying, "Oh my God! We almost lost you! " It was a surgery that was supposed to take 45 minutes. It wasn't until hours later that I opened my eyes. I have low blood pressure. They didn't take that into consideration.

I knew in the sound of the Moyo drum that I had died but I came back.

And yes, they almost lost me. After the Moyo drum incident I spoke with my current doctor (not the surgeon) and related the experience. He said yes, that is what happened... I know my heart had stopped.

For years that time of death has been blank like a black covered window. I couldn't remember what happened. I couldn't peer inside. A few people asked if I had seen light or or or. I shook my head.

Lately I have wondered about my life. I ponder on the purpose and a weariness that is upon me. I am a sensitive, a contemplative sort and today, as yesterday, I wonder about the "why am I still here." And then it happened. Today I downloaded yet another zip knowing/vision/epiphany. I was watching as an observer, an occurrence from long ago. It was about that time in the hospital. Only today, a Saturday in August, I now remember. I am like an observer, looking at that time...

My father met me in that place of death. He met me and I told him I wanted to stay there. Life held no more for me. I was ready to be done. I was not depressed or suicidal. I had raised three kids alone, now they were all grown. And I was tired. So very tired. I had worked very hard in this place called life.

My father told me my kids needed me still.

He told me that I have great purpose in that world.

He let me know in that mind-to-mind talk that I wasn't done yet.

Then he confided in me that he had given up too soon.

That he understood tired.

His life was finished, he felt.

The pain was too great. He understood that. And he let go.

He asked me to not let go. He asked me to stay. This was 13 years ago.

What is it that lies before me to accomplish? What is the reason I am still here? Honestly, I don't know. Dear friends tell me I have much to teach and share. Where are the ones who want to hear? If you were to look at my life it may seem like a failure. A well-meaning person's comment yesterday about money certainly brought that up for me. Her comment was all about materialistic gain. To so many that is the goal. They look at my life and see there are needs for house repair, for what I cannot afford. Yes, I am learning about monetary gain. And yet, I am not a failure. I just live in a different place, a place between worlds. And deeper in I go.

I think now about a friend who has seen much pain. He too wanted to leave in the midst of a cardiac bypass. In prayer for him I entered into the room of spirit, to talk with him. I encouraged him in the love of God, with understanding, compassion and said in the knowings, "You have a grandbaby coming. He will need you." My friend never knew about this sacred conversation. He doesn't know except in his deepest heart that has not spoken out loud to him. And I won't tell him. It is of no avail. He stayed. He got better. He is still here and his grand baby is too.

How is this that we go back and forth between worlds? How is this that I am so deeply moved and touched that I sit here weeping as I type? Tears fall down my cheeks. I am sobbing. I am not sad. I am not depressed. They are washing tears.

And I know beyond doubt that God shielded my eyes from seeing the wonderful glory at that that time… Shekinah glory that I have walked in during other moments of my life. If I saw that, at that time, I would not have come back. I know this is true.

That is what happened when I died for that time in a hospital in California. I am watching me in that moment of death and also watching for today, knowing that I'm not done yet. I am now ready for what is next.

11. The Universe Within

Dost thou think thyself only a puny form when the universe is folded up within thee?"-
Abdu'l Baha quoting Iman Ali, The Secret of Divine Civilization

The universe that is folded up within me
    Whispers in the night,
    Tearing down the old beliefs
    That I am merely a puny form.
I look into night sky
Beyond the closest stars that gleam a million miles away
    And I understand
There is more, so much more.

And in curiosity and telescopic examination
    I learn
That which is seen as dark
    Is over three thousand galaxies
    I have never before viewed
    Or known about
    Or even pondered.

Looking into outer darkness to uncover galaxies in the night sky
Looking into inner darkness to understand the universe within
I first move from the form of human in the small world I stand
    upon
Into union with rock, blade of grass, tree and all men.

And now I move beyond my small earth-world view,
    my solar system view,
    my galaxy view and
Into the universe;
Into all that is.

It was but a brief flash, a glimpse, a mere knowing,
    Because I am expanding beyond that old puny form.

It was a glimpse that did not last
And yet this glimpse called me onto the next step...
    It waits here for me.

--Annie Mathias

12. The Day I Died, Part Two
The Homecoming Story

Yesterday I realized that I had created art, years ago, to depict my experience. My subconscious whispered this to me in the night because I hadn't realized this, at least, not until yesterday. I went looking for it, this print that I had created so many years ago, in 2009.

I decided to let this art "speak" to me instead of me speaking about it. In 2004 I was given a process to do this and then I wrote a book about accessing our inner stories. Here I am now, 13 years

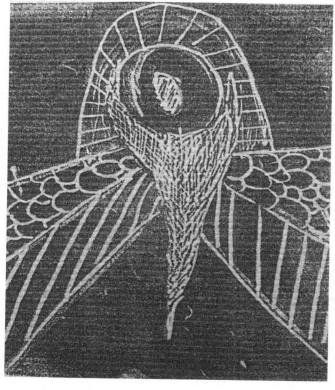

later, using that process. I find this all so amazing and profound. So I step into my own process and proceed into remembering that which I have blocked. I learned to block and repress at an early age. And now I am learning to unblock. And this morning I decided to listen. And this, in the voice of this art, is what it is saying...

I am coming home. I have entered into the realm, that eternal realm, and I am gliding. I can feel the (what do I call it?) calling me, drawing me. I have my arms up and I am so full of all that is around me. I am the music as I move closer. I am the rock of precious worth that lines my walk. They glitter without reserve and the path is certain as I move forward. Here I am without fear, without weariness. I am one with the dazzlement that lies ahead. I am in a full circle with all that is. I belong here. I was created for this place. I am coming home. Oh, I sigh as tears flow. Oh yes. Here is where I belong. I was created for this. And I move deeper and further towards that. It is like a giant arch, a doorway of light. It is the lost city that extends forever. This is where my heartbeat originates. This is where I can breath in living color and my words are no longer needed. The struggle with being is not, not here, because I am one with it all. I am home.

All shame is gone. I cannot even remember what that was like, actually. Except who I am is so very welcome here. I am not weird, or strange. I am, and in the presence of love. I have a body but I do not. There are not any angels with harps. There are colors that I taste. They taste wild, like what a butterfly must experience when it drinks nectar. Or what starlight tastes like. Deep and pure light upon my being and with a crystal like multi faceted echo of flavor that changes, ever so slightly, with each echo. The colors blend and swirl. They are the alien colors that I see in my dreams but not with my eyes open. All the colors are friends with each other; they delight in one another's beauty. There is no competition and so they radiate in order to show their own and each other colors' radiance. And so the flavor of the colors before me is a continuous flow of taste without interruption. I start with the color/taste of what I would describe as the gleaming moss looking stone that erupts in peaceful forest like creamery and how did I end up here, in the vibration of a pulsing orange like orb that allows all of me, whoever I am now, to be drinking in the taste of alive like I have never before known? I slid, or danced, or perhaps flew from one color taste to another, the entire spectrum within seconds or hours? I do not know about time here, I only know now.

And there is the hum harmony. A deep nothingness that is so full I cannot begin to comprehend it. I have heard it before, decades ago, in the singing of angels in an abandoned barn in the midst of a thunderstorm and yet that distant memory allows me to connect like to an almost forgotten dream. I have almost heard this many other times, like when I listen to stars singing. But here there is no effort at all. I do not listen from my ears but from my knowing, my being.

And here I pause. I am sitting on my back porch and grape vines grow upon the overhang above me. In a cast shadow I am aware of a winged one, a monarch butterfly, hovering overhead. I have been in a trance like place, remembering. It is a clearness and power without violence...what is the word for that? I feel like as I write I am transformed, awakening back. Seeing more clearly. Remembering and owning.

And I have not yet begun to describe the love.

But that word, love, is way too small. It cannot hold the deep resonance that is all around me. Like it's always been here. I know, because I know things here without being told, that it has always been here. And I know that it always will be.

The melting away is also here.

But it is not emotional. I do not feel emotional like I normally do. I watch and I understand because my capacity for understanding is more. Wider and deeper. Without any effort. I am like a light here, in the midst of the sun. I am a part of it. I belong. I am breath and I breathe with all that is here. Each breath is an "us" breath. I am aware of being not I but all. How can I explain this to you, perhaps this is foreign. If one part hurts, it all hurts. If one part is joy, we are all joy.

As I write I am as one in a dream. All the ways I am here, in my earth bound life, are mere whispers but in The Homecoming Realm they are/were full out explosions of being. I didn't have to use out loud words because the knowings were how we communicate. I was free from my sorrows. There was no pain. I was so enwrapped in love. It was so real. So real. When I was there, I experienced The Great Melting Away.

I wonder how it is that it took so long to come back to this remembering. How could I not remember? And yet I look at my life after this experience and the evidences were there. I see more clearly. My belief system shifted. I had different dreams. I have always been one with dreams and visions but my life became so much deeper, more contemplative. I am not competitive. Life became about "The Us, The All." It was a time of great shifting and transition. It was indeed The Great Melting Away.

Did I see others that I knew? I already told you how I saw my father. But I also saw my Great Grandma Paul. She and I have always had a special connection.

When I was in Scotland, years ago, I was riding a train that went past Pullmont House where she and her family lived. I looked up and saw a little girl in a faded blue dress; she was about 8 years old, standing on the side of the tracks with a wooden basket of vegetables in her hands. Even now the recollection is so vivid. She looked at me straight in the eye, and smiled at me. I didn't connect fully and understand all of what was happening. Years later I asked my mother about Great Grandma Paul. Were there any stories about her youth? My mother told me that her family, who were caretakers at Pullmont House, had a garden and every Saturday they would send little Annie Paul to market with a basket of vegetables they had grown. She was sent because a child could ride the train for half fare.

Grandma Paul calls me honey. She has white hands that are very smooth. She is here and she takes my hand. *Or in trying to describe this to you now, I can only say that she takes my hand.* And she looked deep inside of me. I love not having to use words. *I am in and out of the remembering now. I have, in my earth body, a deepened understanding of why I choose to write in poetry/story form. My insatiable quest to birth these stories into this realm is so expansive. The words in a poem I wrote,* The Kiln Firing, *floods over me, reaching far beyond my words:*

But I cannot find words or expression to explain
The depth and width of the creative search, long into the night
The why of artists,
Continuing deeper into their art,
Seeking to explain to others
That which can never be contained.

May 14, 2017

13. Blind Spots

Two weeks ago I took my big dog for a walk. Stryder is a rescue dog. We don't know anything about his past so it has been a great time of learning. We were doing really well; we were almost home until the black/brownish dog, the one with the long legs just like his owner, came by. He was on the other side of the street but I could already feel Stryder start to become afraid. And at that moment Stryder did not want to be walking on the outside. He wanted me, his beloved human to be on the outside. This way he feels safer. He quickly cut in front of me. I tripped over him. The concrete isn't very forgiving.

I fell hard. The owner of the black dog, across the street, called over, "You ok?" "Yeah, I just tripped," I said, trying to sound brave and not embarrassed. I stumbled to get up. We were by our driveway so we hurried inside. My left hand hurt, it really hurt.

I got us inside and grabbed some ice and then some hydrogen peroxide for the cuts and scrapes. I began to cry. My now rapidly swelling left hand hurt quite badly. I could tell it wasn't broken but it hurt a lot. When you are all alone and crying, you know it has to be bad.

My tears were out of pain and frustration. I hadn't cried in a long time but today I did. My hand swelled. I worked healing upon it. After an hour I got a handle on the pain. But over the next few weeks my knees, side and hand let me know that I had taken a spill. I am just now able to almost make a fist.

Dr. Packard looked at my eyes on the day of the fall. He is the one who fit me with a strong contact and special glasses so I now have

Ninja eyes. Thanks to Dr. Packard I can now see well enough to drive in the dark. I have depth perception again after many years. And I told him about falling. He looked at me and knowing well my serious eye episode of six years ago his said, "When you don't have your contact on, you have a blind spot because one of your data collectors isn't collecting information. YOUR EYES COLLECT DATA THAT YOUR BRAIN PROCESSES. When you fell you were working at 50%."

I thought about that. He was so right. It now seemed obvious, now that he had put it that way. Due to this serious eye episode, my right eye does not have a regular lens and if I am not wearing my strong contact lens, I am only able to see vague shapes. The other eye has an implanted lens after cataract surgery and sees far. I have a zone with no sight. That is where Stryder was when I tripped over him. I had tripped twice, actually, in these last weeks. No wonder.

Of course the metaphor of blind spots was a big one for me. I have blind spots that cause me to trip over other things. My fears can cause me to have blind spots. They cause me to trip and fall or to not move at all.

I am working on a new online course. I am going at turtle speed. I set aside time and tip toe forward. I know the material. I have taught this course in real time. What is the blind spot? The fear of being seen. It is on a deep level I cannot seem to get past it. How do I overcome a blind spot? By knowing that it is there and practice taking steps anyhow. It may not go away, I may always have this fear, this blind spot, but the more I work with it, the more I will become used to it. I will someday be able to say, "Oh, that's in the zone that I can't see clearly.

But if I could see clearly, this is what I would be able to see:

I would see a woman who is, in one daughters' terminology, a badass mama who has raised three fierce daughters. I would see a woman who has overcome many difficulties and risen past them, a woman who is courageous and honest and strong. She is a loving person who knows that her reason for being here in this world is to be of service. And she is doing just that.

I would see a woman who is ageless. She is talented and also gifted with abilities that she is no longer ashamed of. There are no tasks that she is called to and cannot do, once she applies her heart. She is tenacious and always finds her way. She is a woman of faith. She inspires others.

Having a blind spot does hold blessings. She realizes that she needs a different type of friends; she needs traveling companions who will be delighted for her when she succeeds. She needs ones who will cheer and their eyes will sparkle with joy as she accomplishes her goals. She needs friends who rejoice in her victories as if they were their own. It doesn't matter if her goals are in artwork, in music or in writing, they will delight in her success because they are not small and jealous people. She realizes that most of her "now friends" have been happy to have her be small. They like to call her teacher but do not want this teacher to rise beyond their grasp. They do not really understand the work she does but they somehow know that if she grows, they would feel even smaller so they seek to keep her down. But now, in this place of *Understanding Blind Spots*, she sees this more clearly. And out of the corner of her eye she is aware that something is happening. A new group of friends are forming around her.

Gathering around her are other ones who are also strong. They are not intimidated because they honor and understand their own power. They understand they are hollow reeds for the flowing of various gifts and abilities. She sees them coming, dimly at first. They come out of the vapors and the woodlands, these ones that she has been calling for all of her life. She is starting to be surrounded by others who realize they too are open vessels and she does not have to shrink down, in energy and in skill, to be a part of them. She can stand tall and let out that which would have once been repressed and packed away.

If I could see clearly, I would see what is happening. I would understand that this is a transformation process; it is clearly quite phenomenal. I will tell you also that I have a scar on my right eye from this very serious eye episode, back in season of *Writing With Eyes Closed.* * For a time there was a large black circle in the center of my sight. But eventually my brain reformatted. I no longer see the black circle in the middle of my sight. It will be interesting to see what comes about with this blind spot and how I will not trip and fall but instead, I will learn to fly.

(* *Writing With Eyes Closed* is my next book to be published...)

14. What do you really want in life?

This question calls me and terrifies me. It is the song of the mythical sirens, calling the sailors into an alluring place. This question grows and swells to become all encompassing and compelling, filling not only my ears but also my entire being. I am a sailor under the seductive spell of these sea sirens, this question is the all surrounding sound which draws me like an inescapable, unmerciful magnet, because I, like the sailors, have my mind full of nothing but the stupor of the sound. In this we do not only hear, but we become the essence of this call, I cannot separate the notes as I swirl into the whirlpool that eventually overtakes me. I am Jonah in the belly of the whale, alive and swallowed whole.

What do you really want in life? I hear them ask. Into my entire being they ask, these ones who have joined in the song. In my unspoken understanding I recognize different voices, they are voices of my mentors...

"The most exhausting thing you can do is to be unauthentic", I hear Mary Oliver speak. Her voice rises above the surf and I hear her words spoken over the waters. I know she is speaking to me.

From the reef I hear another voice and even without seeing, I recognize his voice. Henry David Thoreau speaks and his words move past my ears, across the oceans of my being, "Dare to be remarkable. Go confidently in the direction of your dreams." He sits with the sirens, it is a moment of clarity and I do not have the ability to move away. He has left Walden Pond to speak to me now. He does not move his lips to form words because these words are already in my heart. He merely looks at me and I hear without sound. I respond in the motion of a nod that has taken a

53

lifetime to develop.

"In the attitude of silence the soul finds the path in a clearer light, and what is elusive and deceptive resolves itself into crystal clearness," Mahatma Gandhi speaks. It is in this path of silent light that I sit, in the elusive shifting, and I watch as the whirling around me is altered and now becomes a focus that diminishes the beauty of prisms and rainbows. I am here, in this moment, the question quaking in my most naked form.

What do you really want in life?

I think, all in a microsecond, of the answers I would have responded with during various stages of my life. They were answers I believed to be true and fitting and good and I now watch as they crumble before me like dust mites drifting in the sunlight. I watch all this in slow, surreal motion. I am the observer who stands a step away from herself. I seek to turn away and yet I know, I know now that there is no turning away. I am stripped of all previous answers, the ones I have tended for years. They did not taste like excuses that kept me from the true question, no, they were, in their time, true and honorable. I stand in this slow unfolding, knowing that I can no longer hold onto these reasons that were once valid to me. I watch these answers for my life come forward like retired survivors. They stand in a line and I know each one intricately because I have lived each one. I have lived how I must raise and care for my children, teach in churches and prepare food for the hungry. These are the foundation floors of my life that I have I stood upon them, stating in my actions and my words and actions as I hold out my hands to others …. I want to continue on, identifying each individual in the line of my reasons for being, calling them true but no longer my present life. My words are met with the echo of silence, the silence that comes at the end of everything and the beginning of nothing.

I really want to write, I whisper, knowing I do not know the real words.

I want to write beyond my words and translate the lines into that which I do not know how to speak. I grasp for more ways to explain but I only stutter. I want to have the ability to somehow communicate about that which has no words. What I really want is to speak and write and be in the hidden language of the unsaid and the unseen. The silence is more eloquent than my words ever will be. I sit in this wisdom for a moment before going on.

I really want to write, I say again, aware that these words are the

best that I know. I do not know the words to express what it is to be a one musical note that falls into a broken heart, reaching in and coating the damp, cold walls of sorrow; softly touching until the vibration increases: the filling and the being, the reaching to the depths and realms that lie beyond. It is the expression of ancient earth upon the roots of a tree, holding and filling and becoming one. It is the smell of mirth and wisdom and long suffering that somehow transcends into the golden glow of strength and beauty.

I really want to write, I whisper. I want to write in colors that only dreams can paint, in the yellows that are sweet on my tongue like morning love. I want to write in the breathing layers of blues that taste like a bird song, wafting thru my open window. I want to write in that cool, wet green, a liquid so delicious that the reader will tilt the page so the living dew falls rolls off onto a parched tongue. I want to write in deep hues of purple that hums in the magic of nighttime, the dark wonder unfolding, coming alive while the rest of world slumbers.

My writing is not limited to words that form lines upon a linear page. This writing is the expression of my heart, the reaching out and holding, the healing, asking, inviting and pulling from places that are not seen into a space where these words become visible and take on life. Like the blind man who begins to see dim forms from darkness or the deaf man whose silenced ears begin to open … the roaring sound wall of thunder begins to change, to transform into a specific song, a taming, a becoming of clarity and precise tone…

My writing is calling into the closed spaces. It is opening doors of wonder that are locked and bolted and yet in reality they are only waiting for the vibration of the correct words. These places wait for the writing to call out to them, for the books that have not yet been written to offer this magic a place on the page.

I really want to write, I say, knowing that what I mean is to fly, to be, to twirl into ecstatic dance and call it a poem. **I really want to write,** I say, pausing to understand that no longer is my journal satisfied to hold these pages ... it now longs for dimensions and realms that exceed all my senses and sensibilities. The journals of my life are no longer content to hold pages within covers and remain closed. These pages escape the bound books and I do not run after them. I let the winds carry them ...

I really want to write, I say, in a phrase that once meant one thing and now has completely changed, just as my life has changed and I cannot fully understand what I mean when I say these words. I am caught between words and wonder:

How will I speak in outloud words to sing the songs that surround me?

I wonder how to pronounce the names of the fragrances that fill me. They are wafting over me, they exceed my ability to smell and now fill my heart in a garden of ecstasy. I stand here, in this moment, repeating again the only words I know in an attempt to explain the unexplainable.

I utter slowly the words that I have loved all my life.

I really want to write.

ABOUT THE AUTHOR

Diane L. Mathias is a lover of words. As a life long writer, her words come forth in a myriad of ways. Her One-of-A-Kind books reflect the creative flow that runs deep within her. Her courses in writing as a healing modality (for the bereaved and those who seek transformation) speaks to the strength of this passion.

And then there is the poetry and the storytelling. Mathias teaches how words are medicine. They are baskets to bring food to body and spirit. Mathias tells her students, "When words wake you in the night, you must listen. Words are the vehicles to carry energy, the life force, the ways of our heart. Our words are not complete and so you must learn to talk story, to speak in metaphor and dream speak. You must also learn to sing with stars."

Diane Mathias' life overflows with spiritual essence and creative pursuit. She is active in showing her art at various art shows, playing music, creating and teaching online classes as well as writing. She would love to hear about your voice of real.

You can contact "Annie" (as her friends call her) at:
www.DianeAnnieMathias.com
https://www.facebook.com/WonderPathArt/

What Others Are Saying About The Voice of Real

Diane Mathias has written evocative tales of truth bringing us home to our hidden self. She skillfully blends poetry and storytelling, interweaving words that bring home to us the pain of separation, which we all experience. She never lost her ability to "see true" with her inner senses yet had to learn to keep this secret for fear of retribution from those who were blind to anything beyond the physical five senses. This is her gift to us – sharing courageously her secret stories, allowing us to open ourselves to our own hidden truth. She states it poignantly as she introduces us to the tales about to unfold: "And so my life has been a journey of learning to walk between worlds".

We meet Stryder in the story where she dreams him first. "The dog in my dream became the dog in my life." We meet the woman who always knew she was "incomplete". Who was always sad as a child. Who was never told the whole truth about her birth and what had "really" taken place. The woman whose deep wounding is now transmuted into the gift she is sharing with us here in *The Voice of Real*.

If you would seek to call out, and cease pretending that you fit in and are content with that, I urge you to read, *The Voice of Real*. These stories awaken our own "real voice" as we journey alongside Mathias and discover that her stories mirror our own.

Even though these are Diane's stories, they are ours, because the voice of real within all of us has no boundaries, just different landscapes. The last line in *Mountain Companion in the Rain*, sums it up completely: "Love had called me safely home".

Renette Hinsbeeck-Nel, Bespoke Mentor
Cape Town, Africa
www.rennettenel.co.za

If you've been hiding your Light with fear of being "seen" and ridiculed, this book is for you. Diane shares so authentically and vulnerably many stories from her life where her "gifts" were not only unappreciated, but caused her a great deal of pain. Once I started reading, "The Voice of Real," I couldn't put it down. I didn't want the stories to end. Every story touched me deeply and I know they will touch the heart of anyone who reads them. Thank you, Diane for your courage in giving us a glimpse of your journey and inspiring us to share our own "voices of real" with one another.

Marisa Ferrer, Colombia, South America
#1 International Best Selling Author of
"Magnify Your Magnificence: Your Pathway to the Life &
Relationships You Truly Desire"
MagnifyYourMagnificence.com
MarisaFerrera.com

****

"The Voice of Real" must be savored by those who know they are empaths, those who have always felt like the "outsider", and those creatives who want to connect on a metaphysical level with their "tribe." From the first few lines of the introduction, Diane joins us on a journey to our interconnectedness with life and others. These are threads woven with miracles, magic, emotions, the senses and the heart. Her creative journey, forged in the kiln of life--expresses itself in words as descriptive and eloquent as the music she creates. These are stories to be savored, like an evening with a good friend.

Nicole Mignone, Stuttgart, Germany
Guiding You to Transform Body, Mind & Business
www.nicholemignone.com

What Others Are Saying About The Voice of Real (cont.)

The Voice of Real will connect so many to their own voices. Reading *The Voice of Real* was like returning home to find another room in my house I did not know existed. As I wandered around the room I recognized the stories within, not as mine but stories on a similar plane to my own. The stories and poems about Mathias' life experiences led me along a path that made me want to keep going, to move from one to another, pulled along with curiosity by her words.

The resonance of the stories and poems connected me to feelings of being out of place and defeat as I remembered my own efforts to assist. Throughout this book I was also aware of a quiet determination, many times very deep down where it felt safe, but none-the-less powerful. And as Diane's words, 'I really want to write' appeared on the page again and again I felt my own recognition of the very same.

--Lauren Riesner *is a coach who listens to your words and reveals the hidden meaning within them, allowing you to understand where your obstacles are and what you need to do to overcome them.*
www.perceptionanxiety.com

****

The Voice of Real is a fascinating collection of stories with a central theme – finding the courage to be your authentic self. The author takes us on a journey from needing to hide who she is to celebrating her authentic self and using her gifts to benefit herself and others. We all have gifts and abilities and the challenge lies in accepting these gift and learning to use these abilities even when faced with great fear and discomfort. Therein lies your strength and courage. The author demonstrates this throughout the book by relaying her stories and experiences. *The Voice of Real* will touch your heart and challenge your thoughts about what is considered "normal" in our society.

SM Hannon, MSW, LCSW
The Questioning Years
The Awakening Years
www.smhannon.wordpress.com

Made in the USA
Middletown, DE
28 September 2019